LEARN HOW TO MAKE

Balloon
Animals

Learn How To Make Balloon Animals

First published in 2010 by
SpiceBox ™
3918 Kitchener Street
Burnaby, BC, Canada

ISBN 10: 1-926567-69-2
ISBN 13: 978-1-926567-69-3

CEO and Publisher: Ben Lotfi
Writer: Clare Hibbert
Illustrator: Trudi Webb
Editor: AnnMarie MacKinnon
Creative Director: Garett Chan
Art Director: Christine Covert
Designer: Leslie Irvine
Production: James Badger
Sourcing: Janny Lam

Printed in China

Contents

Fun With Balloons

Anyone can make balloon models! All you need is a bit of practice, some special, sausage-shaped balloons—and clear instructions like the ones in this book.

To get started, you will need modeling balloons and a balloon pump. Modeling balloons are made to be twisted into all sorts of shapes. This book shows you how to create 20 cute balloon animals, using the most popular size of modeling balloon. You can buy modeling balloons from specialty toy or magic shops. Just ask for size 260E.

Some other things you will need are a ruler or measuring tape and some permanent marker felt-tips (water-based ones won't work). It might also be fun to have some stickers or other decorations so you can make your balloon animals extra special.

Using a Pump

Modeling balloons are much harder to blow up than normal balloons. It's not a good idea to try. That's why it's important to have a balloon pump. Before you inflate a balloon, stretch and warm it in your hands. This will make it more flexible. Then slide the neck of the balloon onto the pump's nozzle—and get pumping!

Tying the Knot

Inflate the balloon until it's the right length—check the instructions for the animal you want to make. Then carefully slide the balloon off the nozzle, pinching the neck so that no air escapes. Squeeze some of the air up the balloon a bit, so there's plenty of neck. Tie into a firm knot. Now you're ready to get twisting!

Balloon Know-How

• Store balloons in an airtight plastic box, somewhere cool and dark.

• Trim your fingernails so they don't snag on balloons and burst them.

• Always use a pump to inflate modeling balloons.

• Keep balloons and bits of burst balloon away from pets and small children.

Do the Twist

To make any model, you need to know how to make a balloon bubble that won't untwist. Here's how to do your first lock twist.

Step 1

Hold the inflated balloon with your left hand at the knot end. Using the thumb and forefinger, press down on the balloon about 4 inches (10 cm) from the knot end.

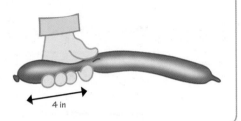

Step 2

Hold the rest of the balloon in your right hand. Use this to twist the balloon twice round. Shuffle your left hand along a bit so that it holds the balloon at the twist and stops it from untwisting.

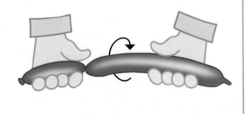

Step 3

Move your right hand along the balloon. Using the thumb and forefinger, press down on the balloon about 4 inches (10 cm) from the first twist. Make two full turns again.

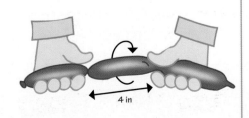

step 4

Being careful not to let either bubble untwist, use your right hand to make a third bubble. Quickly fold this back so it is next to the second bubble.

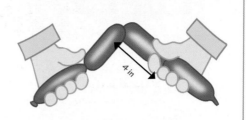

step 5

Still holding the first bubble with your left hand, use the right hand to twist together the first twist and the third twist. After two full turns they will lock together. Now you can let go.

The FOLD TWiST

There is another way to lock twist, and you can do it with just two bubbles. First twist one bubble, then twist another that is twice as long. Fold the second bubble over, then lock twist together the first and second twists. Simple!

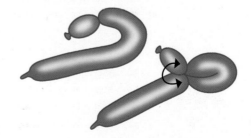

Now you're ready to start modeling!

Puppy

Looking for a cute pet? This little puppy's sure to impress! It's also just about the easiest balloon sculpture to make. Heel, Rover!

Inflate the balloon until it is 20 inches (50 cm) long, then tie the knot.

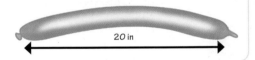

20 in

Twist a 2 inch (5 cm) bubble for the head and two 2 inch (5 cm) bubbles for the ears.

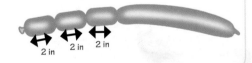

2 in 2 in 2 in

Fold over the two bubbles for the ears and lock twist together.

Twist three more 2 inch (5 cm) bubbles for the neck and two front legs.

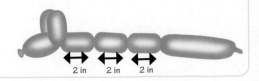

2 in 2 in 2 in

step 5

Fold over the two front legs and lock twist them together.

step 6

Twist three more 2 inch (5 cm) bubbles for the body and two back legs.

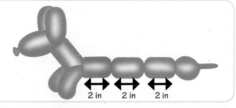

2 in   2 in   2 in

step 7

Lock twist the two back legs together. The leftover balloon makes the tail.

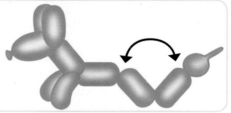

step 8

Use stickers or a marker to add a pair of puppy dog eyes. Draw the mouth on in felt-tip.

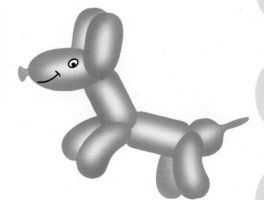

Horse

Giddy-up! You can adapt the basic dog shape to make this cool horse —it just needs smaller ears and a longer neck and legs. Whoa, there!

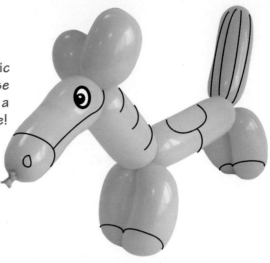

Step 1	Inflate the balloon until it is 30 inches (75 cm) long, then tie the knot— but not too tightly.	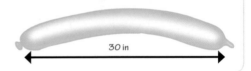

Step 2	Twist a 3 inch (8 cm) bubble for the head and two 1 inch (3 cm) bubbles for the ears. Lock twist the ears.	

Step 3	Pull the knot and roll it to the end of the balloon, until it is tight.	

Step 4	Squeeze the head bubble so that air bulges down at the nose end.	

step 5

Twist a 3 inch (8 cm) bubble for the neck and two 4 inch (10 cm) bubbles for the front legs. Lock twist the legs.

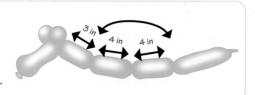

step 6

Twist a 3 inch (8 cm) bubble for the body and two 4 inch (10 cm) bubbles for the back legs. Lock twist the legs again.

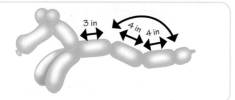

step 7

Squeeze the air in the leftover bubble so that it fills out the tail.

step 8

Stick on some eyes and draw nostrils. Add lines for the mane and tail—and how about a neat saddle?

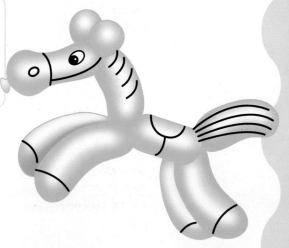

Giraffe

Walk tall with this great giraffe! The front legs are a bit longer than the back ones, so the giraffe seems to stretch up to the treetops.

Step 1

Inflate the balloon until it is 30 inches (75 cm) long, then tie the knot.

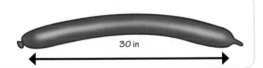

30 in

Step 2

Twist a 4 inch (10 cm) bubble for the head and two 1 inch (3 cm) bubbles for the ears.

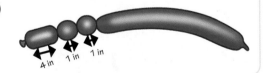

4 in 1 in 1 in

Step 3

Fold over the two ear bubbles and lock twist together.

Step 4

Twist a long, 8 inch (20 cm) bubble for the neck and two 4 inch (10 cm) bubbles for the front legs.

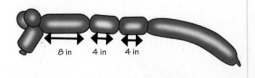

8 in 4 in 4 in

step 5

Fold over the two front legs and lock twist together.

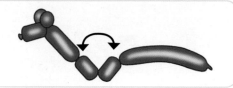

step 6

Twist a 2 inch (5 cm) bubble for the body and two 3.5 inch (9 cm) bubbles for the back legs.

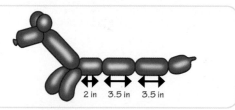

step 7

Lock twist the back legs. The leftover balloon is the giraffe's tail.

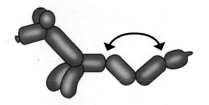

step 8

Stick on some eyes. Draw a mouth and nose for your giraffe, as well as patches all over its body.

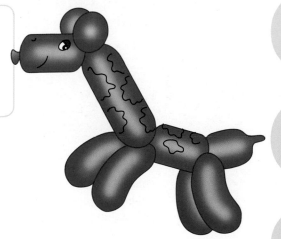

RaBBit

Rabbits make great pets—and if you keep balloon bunnies, you won't even need to clean out their hutch.

step 1

Inflate the balloon until it is 31 inches (80 cm) long, then tie the knot.

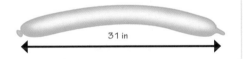

31 in

step 2

Twist a 1 inch (3 cm) bubble for the head and two 8 inch (20 cm) bubbles for the ears.

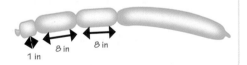

1 in   8 in   8 in

step 3

Fold over the two bubbles for the ears and lock twist together.

step 4

Twist a 1 inch (3 cm) bubble for the neck and two 2.5 inch (6cm) bubbles for the front legs.

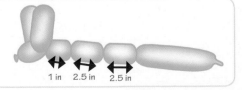

1 in   2.5 in   2.5 in

14

Step 5

Lock twist the two front legs together.

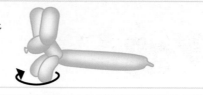

Step 6

Twist three more 2.5 inch (6cm) bubbles for the body and two back legs.

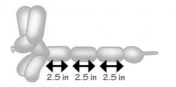

2.5 in   2.5 in   2.5 in

Step 7

Lock twist the two back legs together. The leftover balloon makes a little bobtail.

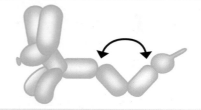

Step 8

Stick on a pair of eyes. Draw your rabbit's mouth and whiskers, then add insides to the ears.

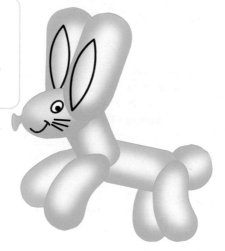

Mouse

This balloon sculpture squeaks more than most! Whatever you do, don't let any balloon cats near this tiny, defenceless little mouse.

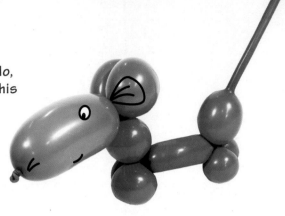

Step 1

Only inflate the balloon until it is about 8 inches (20 cm) long, then tie the knot.

8 in

Step 2

Twist a 1.5 inch (4 cm) bubble for the head and two .75 inch (2 cm) bubbles for the ears.

.75 in

1.5 in   .75 in

Step 3

Fold over the two bubbles for the ears and lock twist together.

Step 4

Pull the balloon downwards at the knot end, to give the mouse a pointy-looking face.

Step 5

Twist three more .75 inch (2 cm) bubbles—for the neck and two front legs. Lock twist the two front legs together.

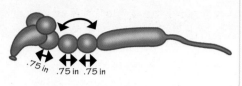

Step 6

Twist a 1 inch (3 cm) bubble for the body and two .75 inch (2 cm) bubbles for the back legs.

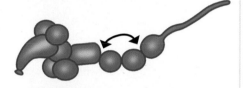

Step 7

Lock twist the two back legs together. The leftover balloon makes the mouse's long tail.

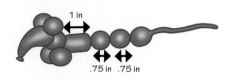

Step 8

Choose a pair of eye stickers, then finish off with more details in felt-tip marker.

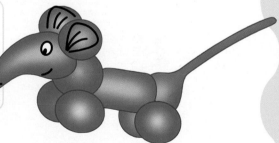

Rhinoceros

Some people believe that rhinos' horns have special powers—and this is certainly a magical model! Start sculpting this one at the tail end.

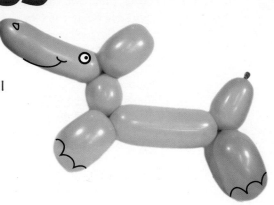

step 1
Inflate the balloon until it is 30 inches (80 cm) long, then tie the knot.

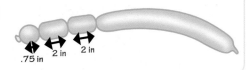

30 in

step 2
Twist a .75 inch (2 cm) bubble for the tail and two 2 inch (5 cm) bubbles for the back legs.

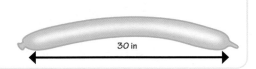

.75 in   2 in   2 in

step 3
Now lock twist the two back legs together.

step 4
Twist a 2 inch (5 cm) bubble for the body and two more 2 inch (5 cm) bubbles for the front legs.

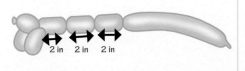

2 in   2 in   2 in

step 5

Lock twist the rhino's front legs together.

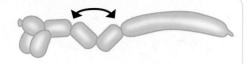

step 6

Twist a .75 inch (2 cm) bubble for the neck and two 1 inch (3 cm) bubbles for the ears. Lock twist the two ears together.

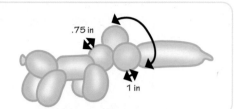

.75 in

1 in

step 7

The leftover balloon makes the head and horn. Squeeze near the horn and pull up until the horn points upwards.

step 8

Add eyes, nostrils and a mouth, using stickers and felt-tips. How about some big toenails, too?

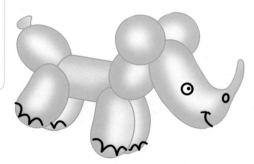

PooDle

Poodles are the most pampered pooches. No wonder this stylish balloon sculpture is always so popular!

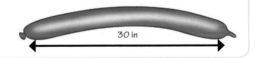

Step 1

Inflate the balloon until it is 30 inches (80 cm) long, then tie the knot.

30 in

Step 2

Twist a 6 inch (15 cm) bubble for the head and an 8 inch (20 cm) long bubble for the ears.

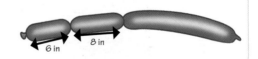

6 in   8 in

Step 3

Bend the ear bubble to form a loop and lock twist.

Step 4

Now bend over the head bubble and carefully poke it through the ear loop.

Step 5

Twist a .75 inch (2 cm) bubble for the neck and two 4 inch (10 cm) bubbles for the front legs. Lock twist the legs.

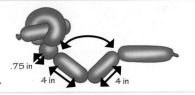

Step 6

Twist a 2.25 inch (6 cm) bubble for the body and two 4 inch (10 cm) bubbles for the back legs. Lock twist the back legs.

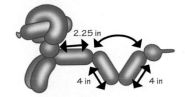

Step 7

Press in the middle of the leftover bubble to force some air into the pointed end. This makes the poodle's fancy tail.

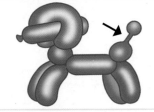

Step 8

Add eye stickers and draw on the mouth. You could color in a couple of pretty bows, too!

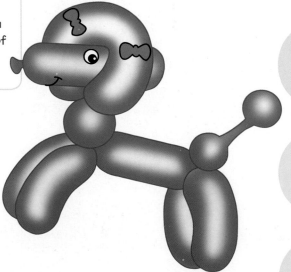

21

Bee or Bird

This model's a real high-flier—whatever you choose as the end result! Decide between a sweet hummingbird or a striped bee.

Step 1

Inflate the balloon until it is 30 inches (80 cm) long, then tie the knot.

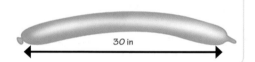

30 in

Step 2

Twist a 2 inch (5 cm) bubble at the knot end and a 2.25 inch (6 cm) bubble at the pointy end. Don't let go!

2 in   2.25 in

Step 3

Bend the whole balloon to form a loop and lock twist the two bubbles together.

Squeeze the middle of the loop, as if you were making a heart, then lock twist to form a pair of wings.

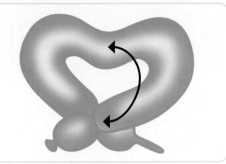

Is your balloon sculpture a bee? Create a face at the knot end and draw stripes across the body. The pointy end is its stinger!

Have you made a hummingbird? The pointy end can be the bird's beak. Stick on eyes and draw in some tail feathers.

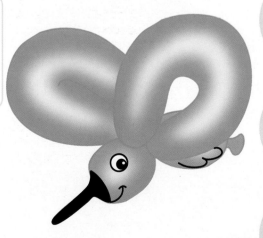

Butterfly

Choose a brightly-colored balloon for this summery butterfly. It has cute, heart-shaped wings and is really easy to make.

Step 1

Inflate the balloon until it is 30 inches (80 cm) long, then tie the knot.

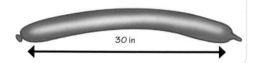

30 in

Step 2

Twist a 2 inch (5 cm) bubble at the knot end and a 4 inch (10 cm) bubble at the pointy end. Don't let go!

2 in

4 in

Step 3

Bend the whole balloon to form a loop and lock twist the two bubbles together.

step 4

Squeeze the middle of the loop, as if you were making a heart, then lock twist to form a pair of wings.

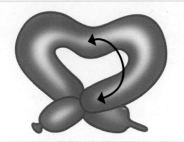

step 5

Shape one of the wings into a heart by squeezing the middle of the loop, pushing out the air and holding for a moment.

step 6

Repeat with the other wing. Now adjust the wings so that your butterfly looks like it's flying.

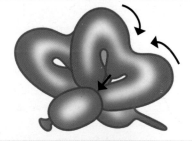

step 7

Stick on eyes and add details to the wings and face in felt-tip.

Dachshund

Dachshunds are nicknamed 'wiener dogs' because of their body shape—not what they eat! Just make a dog with a very long middle.

step 1	Inflate the balloon until it is 25.5 inches (60 cm) long, then tie the knot.	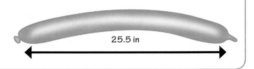 25.5 in
step 2	Twist a 2.25 inch (6 cm) bubble for the head and two more 2.25 inch (6 cm) bubbles for the ears.	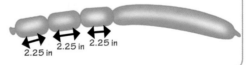 2.25 in 2.25 in 2.25 in
step 3	Fold over the two bubbles for the ears and lock twist together.	
step 4	Twist three 1.5 inch (4 cm) bubbles for the neck and front legs. Lock twist the front legs.	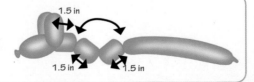 1.5 in 1.5 in 1.5 in

Step 5

Twist a long 8 inch (20 cm) bubble for the body and two 1.5 inch (4 cm) bubbles for the back legs.

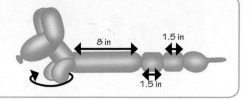

Step 6

Lock twist the back legs together. The leftover balloon makes the tail.

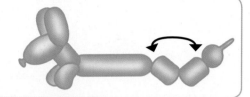

Step 7

Give your dachshund floppy ears. Gently pull apart the ears, then tuck the head and neck in between them.

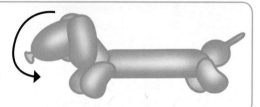

Step 8

Don't forget to stick on some eyes and draw on a smiling mouth!

Parrot

Pretty Polly! You're just a few balloon twists away from having your own pet parrot!

Step 1

Inflate the balloon until it is 30 inches (80 cm) long, then tie the knot.

30 in

Step 2

Twist a 1.5 inch (4 cm) bubble for the beak and two 2 inch (5 cm) bubbles for the sides of the parrot's head.

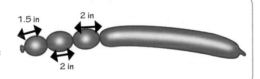

1.5 in   2 in

2 in

Step 3

Lock twist the head bubbles.

Step 4

Tie the balloon knot to the twist at the top of the head.

Step 5

Twist two 6 inch (15 cm) wing bubbles, then lock twist to the head.

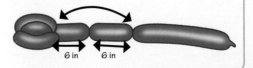

6 in   6 in

step 6

Twist a 6 inch (15 cm) body bubble and two 1.25 inch (3 cm) feet bubbles. Lock twist the feet bubbles.

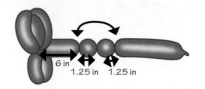

6 in   1.25 in   1.25 in

step 7

Now push the tail through the wings, then lock the feet to the bottom of the wings.

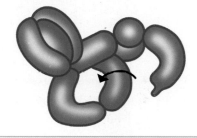

step 8

The leftover balloon makes the tail. Squeeze the air to fill the end and bend the tail downwards.

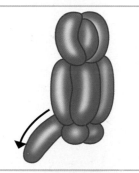

step 9

Stick on or draw eyes. Add a beak and feathers in felt-tip marker. For a perch, loop a second balloon and lock twist it to the parrot's feet.

CoBRa

This snake model's a real charmer! You need to inflate the balloon cleverly to create the spiral shape of its body. S-s-s-super!

Step 1

Inflate a balloon all the way, then let out all the air. This will lengthen the balloon and make it easier to work with.

Step 2

Tuck the tail end of the balloon between your index and middle finger. Coil the rest of the balloon around both fingers, without overlapping it.

Step 3

Carefully inflate the balloon around your fingers, to form a tight spiral. Then tie the knot.

Step 4

Twist two 2 inch (5 cm) bubbles for the head and neck, and a 4 inch (10 cm) bubble for the hood.

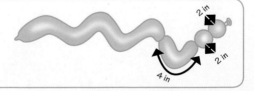

2 in
2 in
4 in

30

STEP 5

Make the hood into a loop and lock twist.

STEP 6

Push the head bubble through the hood loop.

STEP 7

Stick on eyes—try making them yellow. Add extra snaky features in felt-tip, such as fangs and scaly markings.

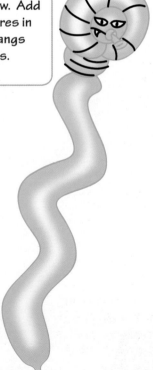

Swan

You'll need a couple of balloons for this great swan sculpture. You can float it in the bath, as long as the water's cool!

Step 1

Inflate both balloons to around 35 inches (90 cm) and knot each one.

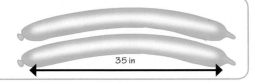

35 in

Step 2

Bend the first balloon into a circle and tie the pointed end to the knot end.

Step 3

Twist the balloon in the middle to make a figure eight. Bend the loops so they curve as shown.

Step 4

Carefully bend over the loop with the knot so that it tucks inside the other loop.

Step 5

Take the second balloon. Twist a 6 inch (15 cm) tail bubble and lock twist to the knot of the first balloon.

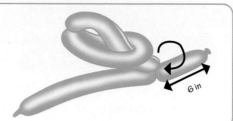

6 in

Step 6

Twist an 8 inch (20 cm) body bubble and lock twist to the central twist of the first balloon.

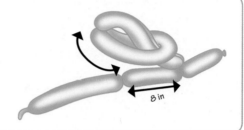

8 in

Step 7

Press in the swan's neck to create a shapely curve. The pointed end is the beak.

Step 8

Stick on some eyes and add lines for the feathers if you like.

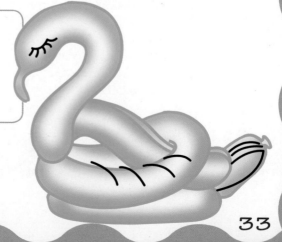

OCtOPUS

You need four balloons for this crazy octopus. Letting out a little air softens the balloons so that they're easier to work with.

Step 1

Inflate three balloons as far as you can, let out some air, then tie the knots.

Step 2

Take all three balloons and lock twist them together at the middle.

Step 3

Fold the balloons, so the twist is at the top. Lock twist again, 10 inches (25 cm) down from the top, to make the octopus' head.

10 in

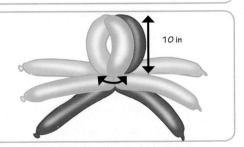

Step 4

Inflate the fourth balloon until it is 30 inches (80 cm) long and tie the knot.

30 in

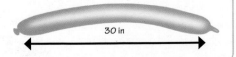

step 5

Twist a 10 inch (25 cm) leg bubble and a 4 inch (10 cm) eye bubble. Loop the eye over and lock twist.

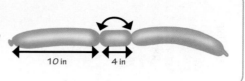

10 in   4 in

step 6

Twist a 2 inch (5 cm) bubble and another 4 inch (10 cm) eye bubble. Loop the eye over and lock twist.

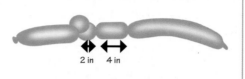

2 in   4 in

step 7

Feed the balloon through the head, so that the eyes poke out. Lock twist the new legs to the others and tuck inside the head.

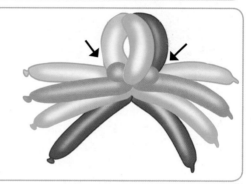

step 8

Add stickers for eyes. You could draw suckers on the tentacles, too!

Dinosaur

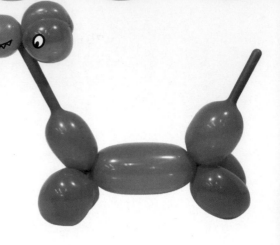

With its weird long neck and boggly eyes, this balloon model looks just like a baby dinosaur. Let's hope it's not a meat-eating one!

Step 1

Inflate the balloon to just 10 inches (25 cm) long, then tie the knot.

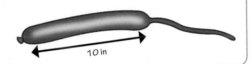

10 in

Step 2

Twist a 1.5 inch (4 cm) bubble for the nose and two .75 inch (2 cm) bubbles for the eyes.

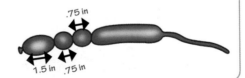

.75 in
.75 in
1.5 in   .75 in

Step 3

Lock twist the eye bubbles.

Step 4

To make the neck, squeeze all of the air out of the balloon for 2 inches (5 cm).

2 in

step 5

Twist a .75 inch (2 cm) bubble at the end of the neck, then two 1.25 inch (3 cm) bubbles for the front legs.

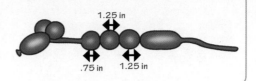

step 6

Lock twist the front legs.

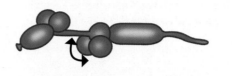

step 7

Twist a 2 inch (5 cm) bubble for the body and two 1.25 inch (3 cm) bubbles for the back legs.

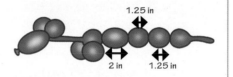

step 8

Lock twist the back legs.

step 9

Stick on eyes, then draw on the mouth, nostrils—and maybe some spines, plates or scales.

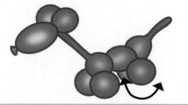

Elephant

You'll need to master the fold twist to make the elephant's enormous ears. Give it a go—the head of the herd is calling!

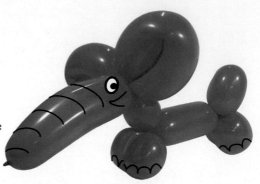

Step 1

Inflate the balloon until it is 35 inches (90 cm) long, then tie the knot.

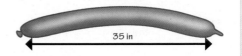

35 in

Step 2

Twist an 8 inch (20 cm) bubble for the trunk and head and another 8 inch (20 cm) bubble for an ear.

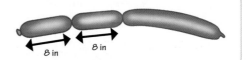

8 in   8 in

Step 3

Bend the ear bubble into a loop and lock twist to the head.

Step 4

Repeat with another 8 inch (20 cm) bubble to make the other ear.

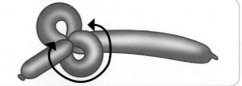

Step 5

Squeeze the trunk hard with both hands to push air into the elephant's head.

step 6

Now bend the elephant's trunk so that it points downwards.

step 7

Twist a 1.25 inch (3 cm) bubble for the neck and two 2 inch (5 cm) bubbles for the front legs. Lock twist the front legs.

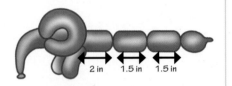

1.25 in
2 in
2 in

step 8

Twist a 2 inch (5 cm) bubble for the body and two 1.5 inch (4 cm) bubbles for the back legs.

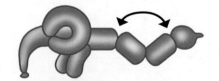

2 in
1.5 in
1.5 in

step 9

Lock twist the back legs. The leftover balloon is the tail.

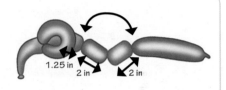

step 10

Add eye stickers or draw the eyes on. Use a felt-tip marker to draw on some long, pointy tusks.

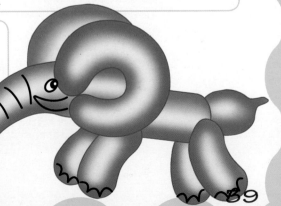

Big Cat

This model can be a lion or a tiger—don't draw the stripes if you're making a lion. You could also add spots instead, to make a cheetah!

Step 1

Inflate the balloon until it is 27.5 inches (70 cm) long, then tie the knot.

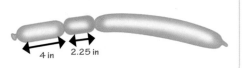

Step 2

Twist a 4 inch (10 cm) nose bubble and a 2.25 inch (6 cm) cheek bubble. Hold these so they don't untwist.

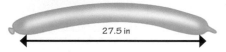

Step 3

Twist a 1.25 inch (3 cm) ear bubble, bend it over itself and lock twist.

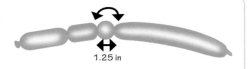

Step 4

Twist another two 1.25 inch (3 cm) bubbles, one for the top of the head and one for the other ear. Lock twist the ear.

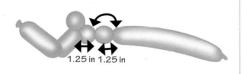

Step 5

Twist another 2.25 inch (6 cm) cheek bubble and lock twist to the nose bubble.

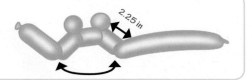

Step 6

Push the nose bubble between the two cheek bubbles.

Step 7

Twist a 4 inch (10 cm) front leg bubble and a 1.25 inch (3 cm) paw bubble. Lock twist the paw bubble.

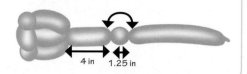

Step 8

Make another 1.25 inch (3 cm) paw and lock twist. Then twist another 4 inch (10 cm) front leg bubble. Lock twist to the head.

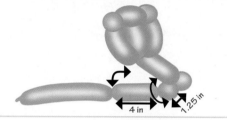

Step 9

Twist a 6 inch (15 cm) body bubble and two 4 inch (10 cm) back legs. Lock twist the back legs.

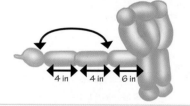

Step 10

To make your big cat sit down, part the back legs a little and tuck the front paws inside the gap.

Step 11

Stick on or draw some eyes. In pen, draw the nose and mouth—and if it's a tiger, stripes!

Bear

This model could be a fierce grizzly bear or a cuddly teddy. You have to sculpt it quickly so the bubbles don't untwist. Grrrr!

Step 1

Inflate the balloon until it is 27.5 inches (70 cm) long, then tie the knot.

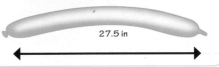

Step 2

Twist a 4 inch (10cm) nose bubble and a 2.25 inch (6 cm) cheek bubble. Hold these so they don't untwist.

Step 3

Twist a 1.25 inch (3 cm) ear bubble, bend it over itself and lock twist.

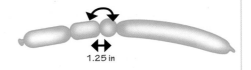

Step 4

Twist another two 1.25 inch (3 cm) bubbles, one for the top of the head and one for the other ear. Lock twist the ear.

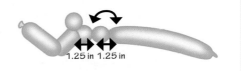

Step 5

Twist another 2.25 inch (6 cm) cheek bubble and lock twist to the nose bubble.

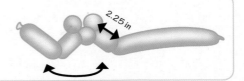

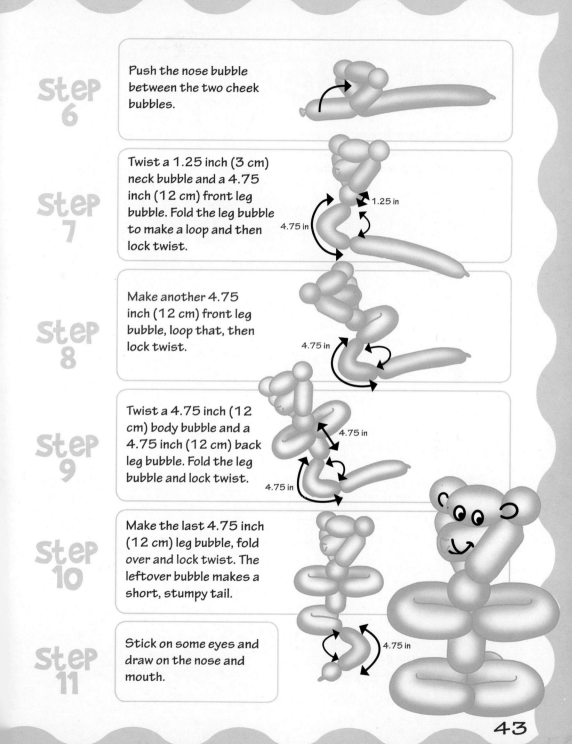

step 6

Push the nose bubble between the two cheek bubbles.

step 7

Twist a 1.25 inch (3 cm) neck bubble and a 4.75 inch (12 cm) front leg bubble. Fold the leg bubble to make a loop and then lock twist.

1.25 in

4.75 in

step 8

Make another 4.75 inch (12 cm) front leg bubble, loop that, then lock twist.

4.75 in

step 9

Twist a 4.75 inch (12 cm) body bubble and a 4.75 inch (12 cm) back leg bubble. Fold the leg bubble and lock twist.

4.75 in

4.75 in

step 10

Make the last 4.75 inch (12 cm) leg bubble, fold over and lock twist. The leftover bubble makes a short, stumpy tail.

step 11

Stick on some eyes and draw on the nose and mouth.

4.75 in

Crocodile

Grab yourself a green balloon and get twisting. Depending on the teeth, this can be a creepy croc or an all-American alligator.

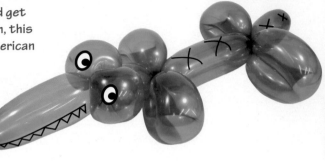

Step 1	Inflate the balloon until it is 33.5 inches (85 cm) long, then tie the knot. 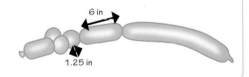
Step 2	Twist a 4 inch (10 cm) bubble for the snout and two 2 inch (5 cm) bubbles for the eyes. Lock twist the eyes. 
Step 3	Twist a 1.25 inch (3 cm) bubble for the neck and a 6 inch (15 cm) bubble for a front leg. 
Step 4	Bend the leg bubble into a loop and lock twist to the neck. 

Repeat with another 6 inch (15 cm) bubble to make the other front leg.

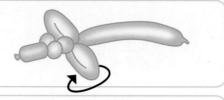

Twist a 4 inch (10 cm) bubble for the body and a 6 inch (15 cm) bubble for a back leg.

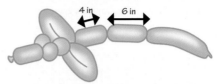

4 in   6 in

Bend and lock twist the leg bubble as before, then repeat with another 6 inch (15 cm) bubble to make the other back leg.

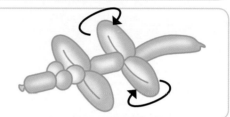

Bend and squeeze the tail so that it zigzags a little. Then add sticker eyes, crisscrossed markings along the back—and some sharp, pointy teeth, of course!

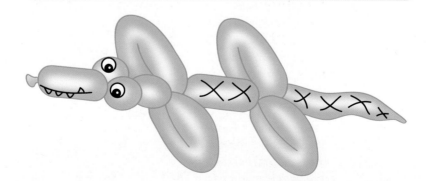

Monkey

You need two balloons to make this cheeky monkey—one for the monkey, and one for the swaying palm tree!

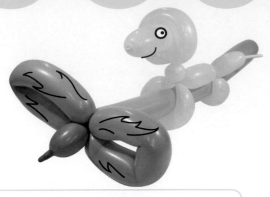

Step 1

Inflate the first balloon to 27.5 inches (70 cm) and tie the knot.

27.5 in

Step 2

Twist a 6 inch (15 cm) nose bubble and an 8 inch (20 cm) head bubble.

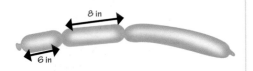

8 in

6 in

Step 3

Loop the head and lock twist it to the nose, then push the nose halfway through the loop.

Step 4

Twist a 1.25 inch (3 cm) neck bubble and an 8 inch (20 cm) bubble for the front legs. Loop the leg bubble and lock twist to the neck.

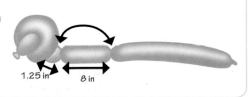

1.25 in   8 in

Step 5

Twist a 4 inch (10 cm) body bubble and an 8 inch (20 cm) bubble for the back legs. Loop the leg bubble and lock twist to the body.

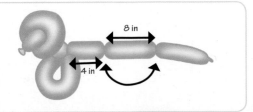

8 in

4 in

Squeeze the air in the tail so it fills the leftover balloon. Stick eyes on your monkey and draw a smiling mouth.

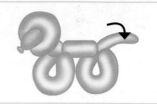

For the tree, inflate a green balloon almost as far as you can and tie the knot.

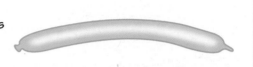

At the end of the balloon, twist a 1.25 inch (3 cm) bubble and two 8 inch (20 cm) leaf bubbles.

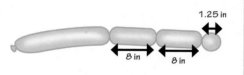

1.25 in

8 in

8 in

Loop each leaf bubble and lock twist to the top of the tree.

Thread the tree trunk through the loops of the monkey's legs.

Star Turn

Ready to put on your own balloon show? Here are a few handy hints!

- Dress up! If you're being an entertainer, you should look the part!
- Don't make too many models. About five is plenty.
- Practice making your chosen models before the show, until you can create them quickly and smoothly.
- Blow up your balloons to the right size beforehand to save time.
- Prepare some "patter"—jokes and funny stories that you can tell to keep the audience interested while you're twisting.
- As you finish a model, hold it up so everyone can get a good look at it.
- Give away your finished models. If you're entertaining at a birthday party, make sure the birthday boy or girl gets the best model!
- Always save your best balloon sculpture for last! It'll be your grand finale.

Happy Ballooning!